INTRODUCTION

Fishing, or angling, is one of the world's most popular participation sports, and is possibly the only one that's equally exciting and relaxing. Anyone, young or old, male or female, can do it, and it is probably the only sport where anyone, no matter how inexperienced, can break a record.

Originally, people caught fish for food, but these days we take great care to treat fish with respect and return them to the water completely unharmed. Catching fish is about learning the skills to outwit nature, and there are lots of hints and tips in this book to help you. Remember, you don't need to catch lots of fish every time to be a successful angler – you just need to respect nature and have a good time.

LOCATIONS & WHAT TO WEAR

Where you go fishing will often depend on where you live and the kind of waters that are local to you. If you're lucky you will have a choice of rivers, stillwaters (lakes and ponds) and maybe even the sea, too.

STILLWATERS

Stillwaters are enclosed bodies of water, like lakes and ponds. They can be anything from a tiny farm pond or purpose-dug commercial fishery, to a huge glacial lake or water-filled gravel pit. The species of fish in stillwaters and the tactics used to catch them vary wildly, but generally speaking, the larger and wilder the lake, the harder the fishing is.

RIVERS

There are a huge variety of rivers to fish. Tiny little brooks may be home to just a few little trout and minnows. Big, powerful tidal rivers contain every species you can think of. You don't have to go to the biggest rivers to fish. Even in small streams there are lots of fish, and some very big ones too.

By Andrew Walker

CONTENTS

● **INTRODUCTION**   3

● **KNOW THE SPORT**

LOCATIONS & WHAT TO WEAR   4-5

● **COARSE FISHING**

EQUIPMENT   6-7

WATERCRAFT   8-9

RODS & REELS   10-11

BAIT   12-13

HOOKS & KNOTS   14-15

FLOATS & WEIGHTS   16-17

RIVER FLOATS & TROTTING   18-19

CASTING   20-21

LANDING A FISH   22-23

LEGERING   24-25

INDICATORS   26-27

● **FLY FISHING**

EQUIPMENT   28-29

CASTING   30-31

DRY FLY FISHING   32-33

NYMPH FISHING   34-35

● **SEA FISHING**

EQUIPMENT   36-37

SHORE FISHING & PIER FISHING   38-39

CASTING   40-41

● **POLLUTION, LICENCES
   & RULES**   42-43

● **BE FIT, STAY FIT**

SAFETY, DIET & FITNESS   44-45

● **HOW THE FAMOUS DO IT**   46-47

● **GLOSSARY & LISTINGS**   48

● **INDEX**   Inside back cover

THE SEA

The sea is a fantastic place to fish. Whether you are lowering a bait from a pier, casting a heavy weight hundreds of metres into a turbulent sea or casting a float off a rocky outcrop, if you happen to live near the sea, you are very lucky!

WHAT TO WEAR

When you go fishing you need to wear some sensible clothes. If it's cold, be sure to wear lots of layers.

WATERPROOFS

Always carry waterproof clothing with you. You never know when it might rain!

DARK CLOTHES

Try and wear dark coloured clothing so that you don't frighten the fish.

FOOTWEAR

Wear footwear with good grip. It can get muddy and slippery by the water's edge. *You could wear trainers or Wellington boots as these have good grip.*

EQUIPMENT

You will probably start your fishing hobby with coarse fishing. 'Coarse fishing' is fishing for freshwater fish which are not 'game fish' (trout and salmon). Coarse fishing involves a wide variety of skills and tactics to target different species, depending on the location, the weather conditions and the time of year.

EQUIPMENT

There is a huge array of fishing equipment (known as 'tackle') available, including rods, reels, lines and all the bits and pieces for all different species and situations.

The type of tackle you use for a day's coarse fishing will depend on where you are fishing and what you are hoping to catch. Here is a typical set-up.

Umbrella

Chair

Tackle box

Bag

Weigh sling

Scales

Unhooking mat

Rod hold-all

Head torch

Catapult

Floats

Hooklength line

Reels

Fixed spool reels

Centrepin reel

Landing net

Carp rod

Barbel rod with quiver-tip

Float rod

Rod rests

Rod bag

TACKLE BOX

Much of the smaller equipment for coarse fishing can be kept in a tackle box.

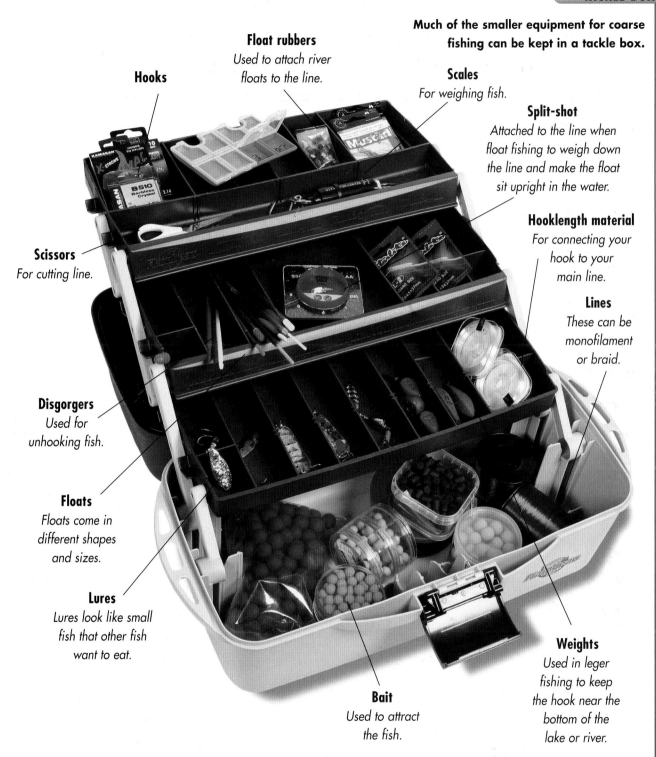

Float rubbers
Used to attach river floats to the line.

Hooks

Scales
For weighing fish.

Split-shot
Attached to the line when float fishing to weigh down the line and make the float sit upright in the water.

Hooklength material
For connecting your hook to your main line.

Scissors
For cutting line.

Lines
These can be monofilament or braid.

Disgorgers
Used for unhooking fish.

Floats
Floats come in different shapes and sizes.

Lures
Lures look like small fish that other fish want to eat.

Bait
Used to attract the fish.

Weights
Used in leger fishing to keep the hook near the bottom of the lake or river.

TOP TIP
It's tempting to take as much tackle as possible for a day's fishing, but try to take as little as you can. That way, it's easier to move to keep in contact with the fish.

WATERCRAFT

Watercraft is your ability to 'read the water', work out where the fish are and how to catch them.

FIND YOUR FISH

Take your time to observe the water before settling into a swim (the place where you fish). If the fish aren't there, you can't catch them!

What to look for
Some fish, like carp, chub and rudd, enjoy basking in the sun. On a warm day you can often see them very clearly. Tench, carp, bream, roach and crucians often roll or jump at the surface at dawn or dusk. Tench and carp also root about on the bottom when they're feeding, sending clouds of mud and bubbles to the surface.

Look for trembling reeds or lilies, coloured water (stirred up by fish on the bottom) and diving birds like grebes (below). These all indicate that fish are in the area.

Bubbles on the surface from feeding fish.

A chub basking in the sun.

A grebe is a type of diving bird.

Fish like cover from overhanging trees, reeds or weedbeds.

PREDATORS

Predators like perch and pike feed on other fish and often strike at their prey, swirling the surface of the water. Remember that predators will be wherever prey fish are, so try to find shoals of small fish by looking for diving birds and little fish near the surface.

WEATHER CONDITIONS

Other things that will help you find the fish are the features of the water, the flow, and the weather conditions. On a stillwater, a strong, warm wind blows emerging fly life and other goodies towards the bank and also warms the water, so it's often good to fish into a wind like this. If the wind is cold, it can chill the water. Then it's usually best to fish in sheltered, deeper areas.

SNAGS

Snags like submerged trees, thick lilies (left) and tree roots all provide shelter and protection, and are especially popular with fish when the sun is bright or if the water is very cold.

 TOP TIP
In rivers, look for 'creases' in the current, where slow-moving water meets faster water. Fish like to sit in the slower water watching for passing food.

RODS & REELS

*T*he huge array of rods and reels available can be bewildering. If you are starting out, the best idea is to visit your local tackle shop with an experienced local angler, or talk to your local tackle dealer about where you want to fish and what fish you want to catch.

RODS

There are rods to suit different types of fishing and their names usually tell you what they are best used for, for example a pike rod or a carp rod.

Most modern rods are made from carbon fibre. The rods come in two or three sections which you push together, making sure that the rod rings are all in line.

JOIN *Where the rod fits together.*

REEL SEAT *The reel is attached here.*

HANDLE *Usually made of foam or cork.*

BUTT *The bottom end of the rod.*

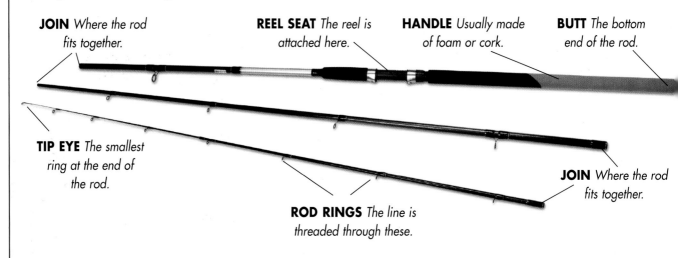

TIP EYE *The smallest ring at the end of the rod.*

ROD RINGS *The line is threaded through these.*

JOIN *Where the rod fits together.*

REELS

There are three main types of reels: fixed spool, centrepins and multipliers.

Bale arm

THE CENTREPIN is a simple type of reel with a spool spinning freely on a spindle.

THE MULTIPLIER REEL is heavy-duty and good for fast retrieval. It is most often used in sea fishing.

THE FIXED SPOOL is the best all-round type of reel. The bale arm wraps line around the spool several times with each turn of the handle, and opens to allow casting.

It is important when loading a spool with line to make sure you load the line to within 2-3 mm of the edge of the spool. Load up at least 100 m of line.

Reel seat

STEP 1

Attach the reel to the rod at the reel seat.

STEP 2

Pass the line through the first rod ring.

STEP 3

Open the bale arm of the reel.

STEP 4

Push the button on the top of the spool and remove it.

STEP 5

Tie the line onto the spool and trim off the tag end.

STEP 7

Wind the line onto your spool, loading it to within 2-3 mm of the edge of the spool. Cut the line and thread it though the remaining rings.

STEP 6

Replace the spool onto the reel and close the bale arm.

TOP TIP

When winding the line on, keep it under tension by holding it with your spare hand between the reel and the rod ring. This makes sure the line is wound on tightly and prevents tangles.

BAIT

Bait is anything you use to tempt a fish into taking the hook. Different species like to eat different things. Always match your hook size to your chosen bait — a big hook with a small bait won't get you many bites. Big bait on a small hook won't hook you many fish!

SWEETCORN
A great bait but fish learn to avoid it on heavily fished waters. Good for tench, bream, roach, rudd, carp and grayling.

PASTE
In water that is muddy or cloudy it is a good idea to coat baits in paste, to give off extra scent.

DEADBAITS
Dead fish are standard baits used to catch pike and zander.

PELLETS
Often used as loosefeed but a great bait for lots of species, especially carp, tench, bream, barbel, catfish and chub.

DOG BISCUIT MIX
These float and on warm days carp will take them from the surface.

WORMS
Worms will help you catch any kind of fish.

CASTERS
Casters often pick out the better fish, especially roach, rudd and tench.

BREAD
Cheap, simple and vastly under-used, bread is one of the best baits there is for roach, rudd, tench, chub and carp.

GROUNDBAIT
A mix of cereals, breadcrumbs and other flavours.

TOP TIP

Whatever bait you use, when you put it on your hook, make sure the point is showing, otherwise you will miss bites.

LUNCHEON MEAT

An excellent bait for chub, barbel, carp, and tench, especially in coloured water.

LURES

Lures are made from wood, plastic or metal and are made to look like small fish that larger fish want to eat.

HEMP

Essential for loosefeed when after tench, roach, barbel and carp.

MAGGOTS

All fish love maggots, from 2 oz roach to 30 lb carp!

BOILIES

These are a good way to avoid the smaller fish and focus on larger carp, tench, bream and barbel.

GROUNDBAIT

Groundbait is a mix of breadcrumbs, cereals and other attractive additives which is mixed with water and put into the swim (either by hand, catapult or in a swimfeeder — see page 24) to attract fish and encourage them to feed.

To make groundbait, add water gradually to the dry mixture and mix vigorously so that it squeezes together but breaks up easily.

Feeding is key to successful angling. You have to feed enough to keep fish in your swim, but not too much so they get full. What you want is a swim of fish actively looking for the next mouthful. That's when you catch them!

HOOKS & KNOTS

H ooks come in many sizes and shapes. The bigger the hook size, the smaller the hook, so a 20 is small and a 6 is big.

TYPES OF HOOK

Spade-end hooks have a flattened area at the top and the knot sits below the spade-shaped flattened end.
Eyed hooks have a small ring at the top and they are tied onto the line with the knot sitting above the eye. Barbless hooks are easier to remove from a fish's mouth and are generally preferred over barbed hooks.

Spade-end hooks

Eyed hooks

Barbed hook

Barbless hook

KNOTS

A well tied knot is essential.
Take your time when tying knots, and always moisten them with saliva before tightening.
Here are some of the best knots to help you when you're out fishing.

TYING A HOOKLENGTH – OVERHAND LOOP KNOT

A hooklength is the short piece of line connecting your hook to your main line.
Always use a lower breaking strain line than your main line in case you get snagged and have to pull for a break. This way you get all your tackle back except the hook.

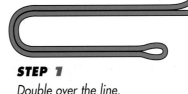

STEP 1
Double over the line.

STEP 2
Make a loop.

STEP 3
Pass the end through the loop twice.

STEP 4
Moisten with saliva, slowly tighten and trim off the tag.
Cut off as much line as you need (usually around 30 cm) and tie on your hook with one of the following knots.

TOP TIP
A really sharp hook is the most vital aspect of your tackle. Rest your hook point on a fingernail and gently pull down — if it digs in straight away, it's sharp.
If it slides across your nail, bin it!

LOOP-TO-LOOP KNOT

Attaching a hooklength to your main line — the loop-to-loop knot.

STEP 1
Tie an overhand loop knot in your main line. Pass the hook (attached to the hooklength) through the main line loop.

Hooklength

Main line

STEP 2
Pass the hook through the hooklength loop.

STEP 3
Carefully pull to tighten the knot.

UNI OR GRINNER KNOT

Use this for larger fish with heavier monofilament or braid line.

STEP 1
Pass the line through the eye of the hook or swivel twice.

STEP 2
Now form a loop with the end of the line and pass it under both lines coming from the hook.

STEP 3
Pass the end down through the loop, around behind the two lines coming from the hook. Repeat this five times.

STEP 4
Moisten with saliva and tighten slowly. Pull the knot down to the eye of the hook or swivel and trim off the spare line (tag).

KNOTLESS KNOT

Use this for making hair-rigs (where the bait is held on a short piece of line tied to the bare hook), when carp, tench or bream fishing, with either braid or monofilament line.

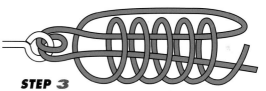

STEP 1
Tie a small loop in the hooklength material and thread your hook onto your hooklength.

STEP 2
Wrap the unlooped end of your hooklength around the hook twice.

STEP 3
Wrap the line around the hook five more times or until it is level with the hook point. Pass the end through the eye of the hook.

STEP 4
Tie a swivel on the other end using the grinner knot (above).

The swivel is a small metal device made of two rings and a pivoting central joint. Line is tied to the two ends and, because they can spin, it prevents the line from twisting and tangling.

FLOATS & WEIGHTS

Weights and floats work together to provide casting weight and bite indication. A float is a buoyant stick-like indicator with a bright tip that is attached to the line and, when set up properly, is the most sensitive bite indicator there is!

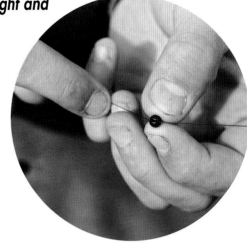

SPLIT-SHOT WEIGHTS

Split-shot weights are pinched on to the line below the float and make the float sit upright in the water.
Split-shot come in different sizes from SSG (very big) to number 10 (very small).

| SSG | AAA | BB | 1 | 4 | 6 | 8 |

Pinching a shot on to the line.

STILLWATER FLOATS

Stillwater floats are attached to the line by the bottom end only, and for this reason they are known as 'wagglers'.
When fishing with a waggler use a float adaptor, which is threaded on the line instead of the float. The float is then pushed into the soft rubber sleeve. This allows you to swap floats quickly and easily without having to re-tackle.

Insert waggler *For close-in fishing in calm conditions.*

Bodied waggler
For fishing further out or in windy conditions.

DRENNAN PEACOCK 2½ AA

Float adaptor
To enable quick changes of floats.

Straight waggler
Less delicate but more stable than the insert waggler.

A float rising in the water, dipping underwater, or moving to the side indicates a bite.

SHOTTING PATTERNS

A waggler floating correctly in still water.

Different shotting patterns make the bait behave differently. Most of the shot for wagglers should be around the bottom of the float, for stability and casting. The remainder is squeezed down the line to sink the bait to the required depth. This is either as a 'bulk', all grouped together, or 'shirt-button' style, evenly spaced down the line.

A bulk is used to get the bait down quickly, perhaps past ravenous tiny fish, and the shirt-button is used to present a gently falling bait to fish higher up in the water. The vital weights are those closest to the hook. These are called 'tell-tale' shots, and are usually very small (number 8 or number 10). With a tell-tale shot 10 cm from the hook and another 20 cm from the hook, any tiny bites will be registered on the float. As the weights fall through the water, they will make the float settle.

You should strike at any movement of the float. Even a tiny lift means you've got a fish.

Correctly shotted shirt-button float.

Correctly shotted bulk float.

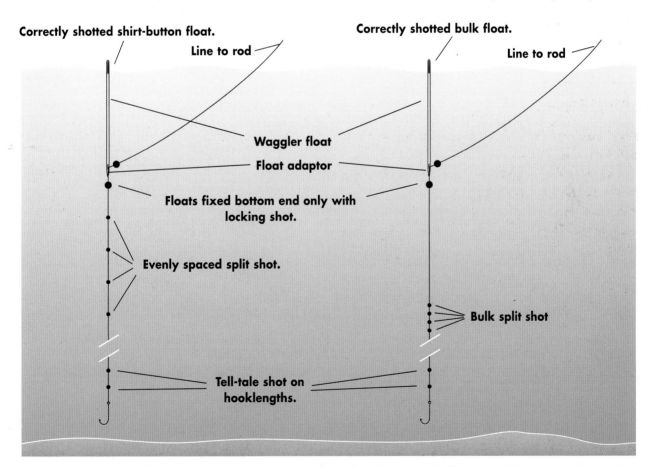

Line to rod

Line to rod

Waggler float

Float adaptor

Floats fixed bottom end only with locking shot.

Evenly spaced split shot.

Bulk split shot

Tell-tale shot on hooklengths.

When you have your float, weights, hooklength and hook in place this is called the 'rig'.

TOP TIP
Take note of how long it takes for the float to settle, including the last tell-tale shots. If it doesn't settle, a fish has taken the bait as the line was sinking, so strike!

RIVER FLOATS & TROTTING

R*iver floats are connected top and bottom by float rubbers, so that they are easier to control in running water.*

FLOATS & FLOAT RUBBERS

Attaching the float with float rubbers means that it doesn't get dragged under by the flow of the river, and it allows you to stop the float moving downstream so that the bait flutters enticingly in the current. This is called 'holding back'.

Float rubbers
Little rubber bands which are used to hold river floats on the line.

Grayling floats
These very traditional floats are designed to be bouyant and visible in fast, broken water where grayling live.

Float rubber

Stick floats
These are delicate trotting floats, used for good presentation in slower, steadier flows.

Chubber floats
These are very buoyant and are a great choice when using big baits or when fishing in very fast water.

Avon floats
These are used in fast water, and their thin stem helps to keep them stable.

TROTTING

'Trotting' is float fishing in running water, controlling the float downstream.
As the float travels downstream, let out line under slight tension so that the float is travelling slightly slower than the current. The flow is much slower on the bottom where the fish are likely to be than at the surface, so this ensures the bait travels at the correct speed. If the hook keeps snagging on the bottom, move the float down towards the hook a little so it's fishing shallower. If it doesn't snag, keep going deeper until you're presenting the bait just off the bottom.

With practise, you can trot a float at just the right speed and guide it into the hotspots where the fish are feeding. It's a skillful, very exciting method!

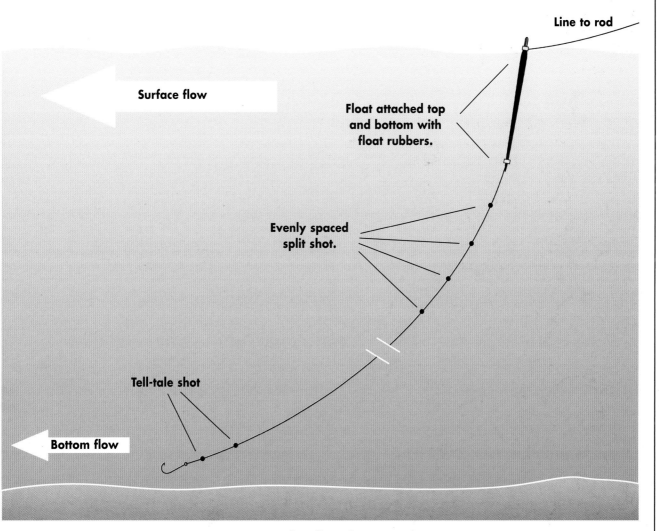

Line to rod

Surface flow

Float attached top and bottom with float rubbers.

Evenly spaced split shot.

Tell-tale shot

Bottom flow

River float rig

TOP TIP
A float taking lots of shot is much easier to control than a lighter float and will therefore present a bait more naturally. Don't be scared of using heavy floats!

CASTING

There are essentially two ways to cast – underarm for close-in and overhead for further out.

CASTING UNDERARM

This is useful for delicate, accurate close-in fishing where a splash may spook the fish. It is also a good way to flick your bait into tricky spots, like under overhanging trees.

STEP 1

Open the bale arm on your reel and let out enough line so that, with the rod pointing up, your rig is at waist height and you have 60 cm of line from the reel to your left hand.

Float

STEP 2

Swing the rig back towards you.

STEP 3

Lower the rod tip, flick the rig towards the water and let go of the line.

Float

Float

STEP 4

Just before it lands, stop the line coming off the reel with your right middle finger. This ensures that the rig lands gently, in a straight line. When the rig has landed, close the bale arm.

TOP TIP
If you can, cast further than you are fishing, and slowly reel in to your spot. This way you are less likely to frighten the fish.

This is used when you need to cast further out.

STEP 1

Open the bale arm on your reel and let out some line so there is about a 1m drop between rod tip and rig.

Float

Float

STEP 2

Hook the line over your index finger on your right hand. Hold the rod with two hands, left hand at the bottom of the handle and the right hand gripping the reel seat and holding the line.

STEP 3

With the rod behind you at an angle of about 45°, pull on your left hand and use the right hand as a pivot.

STEP 4

When the rod gets to 45° in front of you, release the line from your finger.

STEP 5

Just before the rig lands, use your right index finger on the spool to 'feather' the line – this slows the rig down and ensures it lands in a straight line. When it hits the water, stop any more line coming off with your finger and close the bale arm.

LANDING A FISH

W hen you think you've got a bite the first thing to do is to get the hook into the fish's mouth. This is called striking. You do it by moving the rod quickly but smoothly upwards or to the side. Then you need to land, unhook and release the fish as quickly as possible.

LAND, UNHOOK AND RELEASE

Before fishing, set the clutch on your reel so it gives line under pressure and your line won't snap when you hook a monster!

STEP 1
If it's a small fish, you can carefully reel it in.

Clutch

STEP 2
Then swing it to your hand.

STEP 3
Carefully unhook it.

STEP 4
Slip it back into the water.

If it's a bigger fish hold the rod tip high to help tire the fish. If it runs and takes line, keep the rod up. If it heads for a reedbed or other snag, use sidestrain — pulling sideways in the opposite direction — to steer it clear.

Reel in and lower the rod tip. Use the rod to pull the fish in. When the fish is tired and close, hold the landing net underwater and draw the fish over it before lifting.

Carry the fish in the net to your wet unhooking mat.

Remove the hook by pulling gently on the bend.

USING A DISGORGER

Every effort should be made to avoid it, but sometimes a fish may swallow a hook. If that happens you can quickly and easily retrieve it and release the fish with no harm by using a disgorger. Choose a disgorger according to your hook size. Carry several just in case.

STEP 1

Hold the fish firmly but gently with the line fairly tight so that it's between your hand and the hook.

STEP 2

Hook the disgorger onto the line and slide it down into the fish's mouth. Push gently down against the hookhold to release the hook.

STEP 3

Draw the disgorger and hook out, and release the fish.

TOP TIP
If you want to weigh the fish, place it carefully in a wet weigh sling and hang it on your scales. Make sure all its fins are flat against its body. If you want a photo, hold the fish low to the ground and smile!

LEGERING

*L*egering means using a weight or swimfeeder to present a bait on the bottom of the river or lake. There is no float on the line, but there is an indicator on or attached to the rod to tell you when you have a bite. Legering is normally used to present a static bait, and is better for distance fishing rather than float fishing.

SWIMFEEDERS

A swimfeeder is a plastic container with holes in it.
It is used to attract bottom-feeding fish into the area you are fishing. Swimfeeders can be used in place of a leger weight. There are two types of swimfeeder: a maggot feeder and an open-end feeder.

The maggot feeder is filled with maggots before each cast.
The maggots crawl out on the bottom of the river or lake around the hookbait, drawing fish to your bait. Accurate casting is essential with a maggot feeder — you want to hit the same spot each time and build up a bed of feed.

Maggot feeders

An open-ended feeder is filled with groundbait before each cast, which is deposited on the bottom near your hookbait, similar to the maggot feeder.
Again, accurate casting is essential. To begin with, recast every 15 minutes, making sure you hit the same spot every time. It may take some time, but after a while fish will be drawn to the attraction of the groundbait, and you'll start catching!

Open-ended feeder

Main line

Plastic bead

Link swivel

Weight

Hooklength

A running leger is a weight running freely on the main line, prevented from sliding down to the hook by a swivel (onto which you tie your hooklength) and a plastic or rubber bead.

When a fish takes the bait, it pulls the line through the run ring connected to the weight and indicates a bite.

BOLT RIGS

Bolt rigs are a way of legering with heavy weights.

The fish sucks in a bait, swims away and the heavy weight pulls the hook into their mouth making them 'bolt'. There is no need to strike as the fish is already hooked. They are often used when fishing for specimen carp, tench and bream when long periods of waiting are common.

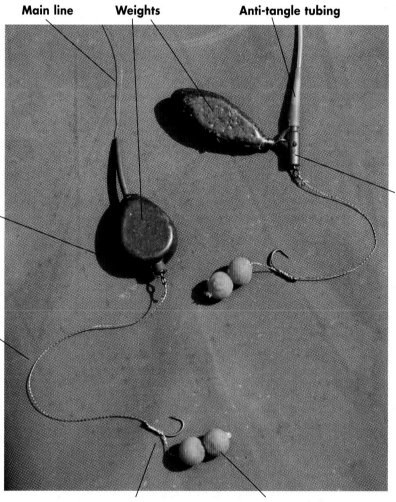

Main line   **Weights**   **Anti-tangle tubing**

Swivel pushed into rubber sleeve.

Lead clip

Hooklength made of soft braid.

Hook tied on with knotless knot.   **Hair-rigged bait**

TOP TIP

Bolt rigs must be 'safe' so that if your line snaps after a fish has been hooked, the weight is able to fall off the rig. If the weight was permanently fixed, the fish would have to drag it around if the line snapped.

INDICATORS

There are no floats on a leger rig, but there are plenty of gadgets to tell you when you have hooked a fish. These are sensitive attachments to the end of your rod or your line that move when a fish is hooked.

QUIVERTIP

A quivertip is a fine, sensitive rod tip which quivers, knocks or pulls right round when a fish has taken the bait.
They can be made of fibreglass or carbon. Fibreglass tips are softer in action and more delicate; carbon tips are stiffer and more powerful. Quivertips are often used when fishing for smaller species.

Bites are indicated by movement of the tip.

Rod rest

Quivertipping is most often used with a running leger or with swimfeeders (see pages 24-25), on both rivers and stillwaters. Once the rig has been cast out, the rod is placed on rod rests parallel to the bank with a 90° angle between the quivertip and line, and the line tightened slowly until there is a tiny bend in the tip. In still water, have the tip as close to the water as possible for maximum indication. In a river, point the rod upwards so as much line as possible is out of the flow.

Bobbins can be used with any leger set-up and are extremely versatile. *They are most often used in stillwaters when fishing for larger fish. Once you have cast out, the rod is placed in two rests (sometimes with a bite alarm) and the bobbin is clipped onto the line between the reel and the front rest. It is set to hang about midway or slightly longer from the rod to the ground.*

If a fish takes the bait and moves towards you, you get a drop-back bite, where the bobbin drops to the ground.

If the fish swims away from you, the bobbin rises to the rod.

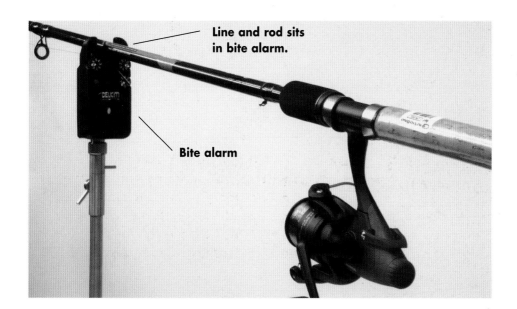

Line and rod sits in bite alarm.

Bite alarm

Bite alarms, or 'buzzers', take the place of the front rod rest and beep when the line is pulled over a small wheel or vibrating plate.

EQUIPMENT

F ly fishing is a way of presenting an imitation 'fly' to catch trout, salmon and grayling, and can also be used to catch coarse and even sea fish. There are thousands of different flies, all designed to mimic the aquatic or terrestrial creatures that fish eat at different times of the year. It is a very active and mobile method and if you haven't tried it yet, you really should — it's great fun!

FLY FISHING EQUIPMENT

6 ft 6 inch number 2 rod

Bag

Tapered leader
A length of monofilament line which is thick at one end and tapers down to a thin, delicate end. The thick end is attached to the fly line and the fly is tied to the thin end.

Reels
Different types of lines and reels can be useful.

Braided loop connectors
This is used to connect your fly line to your tapered leader.

Folding landing net

10 ft number 7/8 rod
On every rod there is an AFTM rating – this corresponds to the weight of the line that the rod will work with.

Floatant
To keep dry flies floating.

Priest
If you are catching trout to eat, this is used to humanely knock them on the head.

Sinkant
To help sink leaders.

Line for tippets
The short length of light line at the end of a leader.

Flies
Dry flies, wet flies, nymphs and buzzers.

TOP TIP
The best all-round set-up for fly fishing is a 9 ft number 6 rod, cheap reel, and a decent number 6 WF, F (weight forward, floating) line.

STEP 1
Attach the reel to the rod.

STEP 2
Attach a braided loop to the end of the fly line. Simply thread the line into the hollow braid and slip the sleeve over the join.

STEP 3
Thread the fly line through the eyes.

STEP 4
Take a tapered leader and tie a loop in the thickest end.

STEP 5
Attach the leader to the braided loop with the loop-to-loop knot (see page 15).

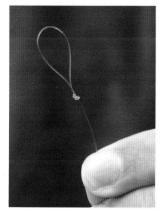

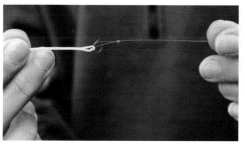

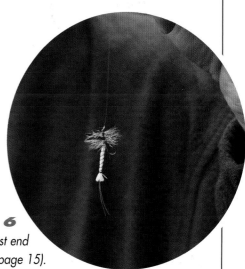

STEP 6
Tie your chosen fly to the tippet (the thinnest end section of the leader) with a grinner knot (see page 15).

LINES

The fly line is very important, and it's worth spending as much as you can afford.
Cheap lines have bad 'memory', meaning they end up in tight coils after being stored on the reel.
There are several types of fly line:

Double taper (DT) These have a long body section with each end tapering to a fine point – good for delicate presentations.

Weight forward (WF) These have a thin body section with a thicker end before tapering to a point – good for casting further.

Shooting head (SH) These are half the length of normal fly lines and are attached to thin backing line – great for real distance casting.

The sink rate of the fly line relates to the speed at which the line sinks through the water, from floating right through to fast sinking.

SINK RATE

Floating These float on the surface of the water.

Sink tip These float, except for the last one to two metres which slowly sink.

Intermediate These sink very, very slowly.

Slow, Medium, or **Fast Sinking** These sink at different rates through the water.

CASTING

*F*ly rods are very flexible, and can store huge amounts of energy. When a fly line (which is the casting weight) bends the rod ready for casting, it's called 'loading the rod'. Strength isn't important, but timing is, which is why practise is vital.

CASTING

When casting a fly you make several 'false casts' before delivering the final cast.
On each false forward cast, a little more line is released, until you have enough line to reach the required distance.

The correct grip.

STEP 1
Pull off enough line for the cast.

STEP 2
Make a back cast. Grip the rod correctly, keep your wrist straight, and move your arm sharply backwards so the rod tip gets to the 1 o'clock position, then stop abruptly. This loads the rod with the weight of the line.

STEP 3
Pause. When the line has straightened out behind you and loaded the rod, move your arm forward sharply to the 11 o'clock position. Let 60 cm of line out with your left hand, and again pause to let the line straighten and load the rod.

STEP 4

Repeat these false casts until enough line is out. Remember to allow a pause for the line to load the rod, and to keep your wrist straight!

Straight wrist

STEP 5

On the final forward cast, let go of the line with your left hand, and as it falls to the water's surface, lower the rod tip to waist height.

Once you've mastered the basics, you can start to get more advanced. When delivering the final cast on a river, try wiggling the rod tip as the line shoots out. This makes the line land in a wiggle, allowing the current to move it without dragging the fly around and making it look unnatural, giving a fish more time to take it.

TOP TIP

Be careful not to allow the fly or line to touch the water until your final cast, otherwise you will spook the fish.

DRY FLY FISHING

*O*f all the methods of fly fishing, dry fly fishing is often considered to be the most skilful – careful observation and accurate presentation are vital. Dry flies imitate terrestrial or emerging insects on the surface of the water. A floating line is used and it can be useful to have some floatant to apply to dry flies, to keep them afloat. The best time of day for dry fly fishing is often the evening, when there are lots of flies hatching.

ON LAKES

Dry fly fishing on lakes is often a case of seizing an opportunity – suddenly a hatch of aquatic insects will occur, or a gusty wind will blow terrestrial insects into the lake, and trout will start rising to feed on them.

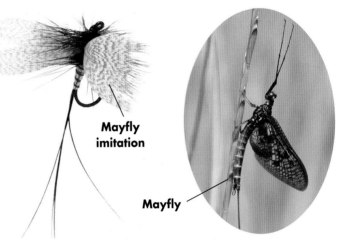

Mayfly imitation

Mayfly

Casting should be kept to a minimum, and you need to be stealthy. Trout will often come very close to the bank if they are undisturbed, which means easier and more accurate casting is possible. Keep the fly as static as possible, and strike as soon as it is taken.

Static dry fly fishing.

TOP TIP

You want your fly to float but your tippet to sink so there's no tell-tale silhouette on the surface. Rub some de-greaser like Fuller's Earth onto the tippet to prevent it floating.

When dry fly fishing on a river, start looking at the most downstream spot and stealthily work your way upstream, watching and listening for rising trout. This way the trout won't see you.

When you see a rising fish, wait and watch – usually it will rise again in exactly the same spot. Next, work out what it is feeding on – you should easily be able to see what flies are being taken. Tie a fly to your line and cast upstream, just above where you saw the fish rise. Hopefully the fish will take it and you'll have a bite!

Cast upstream so that the fly lands just above the point where the fish rose.

NYMPH FISHING

Nymphs are aquatic insects still in their underwater stage before emerging into adults. Sub-surface nymphs make up the vast majority of a trout's diet. Fishing with imitation nymphs can therefore be very successful, but it is also very challenging as trout have plenty of time to scrutinise the fly.

ON LAKES

Nymph fishing in lakes is often fishing 'blind', because you can't see the trout like you can when they're rising to take dry flies.

Getting the fly to the right depth is therefore very important. Start by fishing as close to the bottom as possible, by using a sinking line or a floater with a long leader and weighted fly. Always imagine a fish is following your fly, and try to tempt it with your retrieve of the line. Try small, fast twitches, long slow pulls or a figure of 8 retrieve.

FIGURE OF 8 RETRIEVE

STEP 1
Pinch the line between your thumb and index finger.

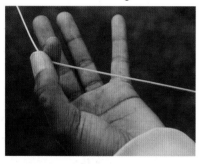

STEP 2
Loop the line around your index finger and your little finger.

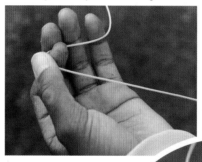

STEP 3
Pull your little finger down to make a loop.

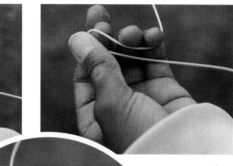

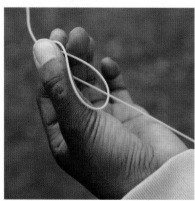

STEP 4
Grab the line from your little finger with your thumb and index finger and release it from your little finger.

STEP 5
Repeat this process to retrieve in a figure of 8.

     TOP TIP
On overcast or warm days, trout are likely to be near the surface.
On bright or cold days, they are often near or on the bottom.

ON RIVERS

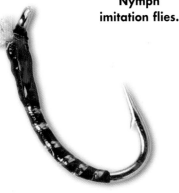

Nymph imitation flies.

There are two ways of nymph fishing a river — upstream or downstream.

To nymph fish upstream, fish a floating line and allow the fly to drift back naturally in the flow, taking up the slack line with your spare hand. To get the right depth, either fish a weighted fly or squeeze one or two small splitshot to your tippet.

If the leader or fly line stops or acts strangely – strike! Takes are often gentle so stay alert.

Fishing downstream is easier because takes are obvious, but the fly looks unnatural as the current sweeps it along. It's better to fish upstream if you can – it's a more difficult and skillful method, but once mastered it will catch you far more trout.

Nymph fishing downstream.

TOP TIP
Explore the river — travel light and try as many spots as you can.

EQUIPMENT

*W*hat could be more exhilarating than casting into the mighty sea? Whether you fish from a sandy beach, a rocky outcrop, a pier or even a boat, there are lots of exciting locations and fish to catch. With some basic understanding of tides, weather, casting and safety you'll soon be fishing effectively and enjoying the challenges of sea fishing.

SEA EQUIPMENT

Sea fishing tackle is designed to be strong and hard wearing to face the rigour of waves and tides.

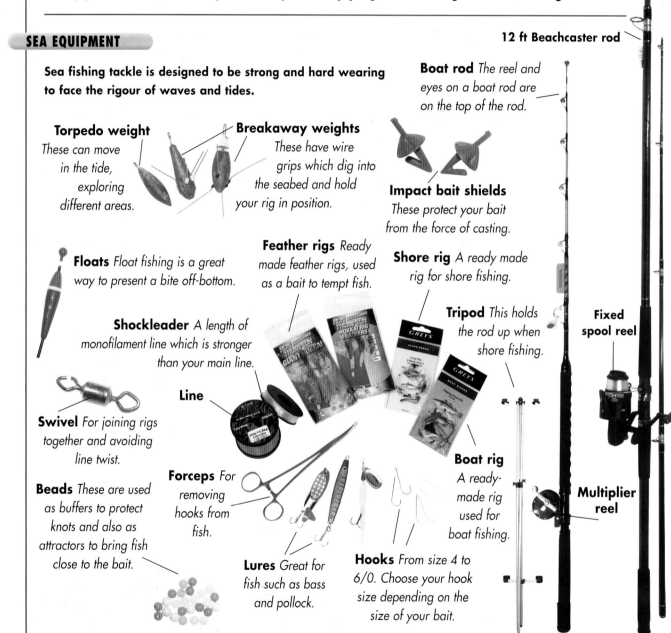

12 ft Beachcaster rod

Torpedo weight *These can move in the tide, exploring different areas.*

Breakaway weights *These have wire grips which dig into the seabed and hold your rig in position.*

Boat rod *The reel and eyes on a boat rod are on the top of the rod.*

Impact bait shields *These protect your bait from the force of casting.*

Floats *Float fishing is a great way to present a bite off-bottom.*

Feather rigs *Ready made feather rigs, used as a bait to tempt fish.*

Shore rig *A ready made rig for shore fishing.*

Shockleader *A length of monofilament line which is stronger than your main line.*

Line

Tripod *This holds the rod up when shore fishing.*

Fixed spool reel

Swivel *For joining rigs together and avoiding line twist.*

Forceps *For removing hooks from fish.*

Boat rig *A ready-made rig used for boat fishing.*

Multiplier reel

Beads *These are used as buffers to protect knots and also as attractors to bring fish close to the bait.*

Lures *Great for fish such as bass and pollock.*

Hooks *From size 4 to 6/0. Choose your hook size depending on the size of your bait.*

TOP TIP

Salt can corrode, so after every trip wash your rod with warm water and a little washing-up liquid and then rinse your reel under warm water.

Bait can quickly go off, especially on warm days. Keep it fresh by keeping it in the shade in a bucket of sea water (change the water regularly) or in a cool box.

Ragworm *A brilliant all-round bait.*

King ragworm *A good all-round bait, these can tempt some big fish!*

Mackerel strips *Cut into strips, mackerel is a very good bait for larger predators, such as bass, rays, tope and conger eels.*

Razor fish *An excellent bait for flatfish, such as flounder.*

Feathers *Mackerel find these irresistible.*

Squid *A tough bait often used to keep softer baits like worms on the hook, but is also a good bait in its own right for cod and bass.*

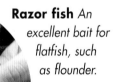

Shore crabs *A great bait for bass, rays and cod.*

Lugworm *A great bait, nearly every sea fish will take a lugworm.*

SHORE FISHING

Whether fishing from a beach or rocks, shore fishing is always exciting. Usual tackle is a 12 ft beachcaster rod and multiplier reel with 15-20 lb line and a shockleader. Good places to cast include sand and mud beds between rocks, deeper holes and gutters around wooden groynes, and channels between rocky and weedy areas.

When shore or pier fishing the rod is held almost upright, sometimes with a tripod, and a bite is indicated by the rod tip knocking or bending over. When float fishing, if the float gets pulled under you've got a bite, so strike!

A rising tide is nearly always the best time to fish. As the sea rises, fish move in to feed on and around the now submerged rocks, coming closer and closer as the tide floods the area. Predatory fish follow smaller fish in too.

Swivel

Crimp
Used for certain rigs to hold hooklengths in position.

Bead

One-hook rig
This is a good streamlined rig for distance casting.

Lead weight

TOP TIP
**Never run on rocks, they can be wet and dangerous.
Always wear good shoes with lots of grip,
and always fish with a friend.**

PIER FISHING

Many anglers begin sea fishing by lowering a bait over their local pier. It's a great place from which to catch fish and to watch the experts.

WHERE TO CAST

As pier structures attract fish all you need to do is lower a bait rather than cast.

It is easier to fish the downtide side of a pier, but you will catch far more if you fish the uptide side. Use a heavy breakaway weight to hold the rig in position. Aim to get your bait close to gutters, or on wooden piers next to one of the pier supports.

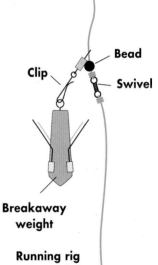

Bead

Clip

Swivel

Breakaway weight

Running rig
The majority of fish feed on the bottom so a simple running rig, with a single hook, is best when pier fishing.

TOP TIP

 At low tide, take note of any gullies, rocks, holes or other features (including snags!) below the pier so you know where to cast when you return to fish.

CASTING

Casting is a skill which is most useful when fishing from the shore, to propel your bait out into the sea where the fish are feeding.

THE OFF GROUND CAST

For long-distance casting use the off ground cast, so called because the rig is laid on the ground behind you before the cast is made.

STEP 1

Face where you want to cast and twist around so you are facing behind you. Put your weight on your back foot. The rod should be about 60° further around. Lay the rig on the ground 90° to the direction of the rod. The distance from the rig to the rod tip should be at least half the length of your rod.

Weight on back foot.

Rig

STEP 2

Open the bale arm and hold the line with your index finger.

STEP 3

Twist back around starting with your head ending with your arms, slowly rising the rod tip. This all compresses the rod and builds up energy. Pull your left elbow (if you are right-handed) up and through and transfer your weight onto both feet.

Turn your body back around.

Weight on both feet.

STEP 4

When your right arm is at full extension above your head, pull your left arm back. The rod tip passes over your head. Put your weight onto your front foot to add power.

Move weight onto front foot.

STEP 5

Release the line when the rod is fully loaded and point the rod at the fast-disappearing rig!

POLLUTION

*F*ishing is about being close to nature, and so comes with responsibilities. Don't leave litter or old line about when you have finished fishing, and remember to close gates properly. Look for specific rules on lakes or stretches of river that you go to and abide by them. Anglers have long been the guardians of the countryside. Often they are the only people to visit more remote areas. Be sure to report any instances of distressed wildlife or pollution you may come across. There's a pollution hotline phone number on your rod licence.

No-one wants to fish in a pond or river like this, so clear up any litter or old line when you leave.

LICENCES & RULES

*F*or coarse and fly fishing in the UK, every angler aged 13 or over needs a rod licence, available from post offices or the Environment Agency website. This allows you to fish with up to two rods at the same time. If you want to fish with three or four rods, you will need two licences. All money from rod licence sales goes to the Environment Agency, who use it to maintain our waterways – so you are directly helping to improve our environment.

UK

Once you have your rod licence, you need permission to fish from whoever owns the water.

This usually takes the form of a day ticket, where you pay a one-off fee for a day's fishing, or a season ticket, where you pay a larger one-off fee to be able to fish a water or selection of waters for a whole year. You can also join a club. This will give you access to a few different lakes and river stretches and you can come and go as you please! Joining a club or buying a season ticket works out a lot cheaper than buying lots of day tickets.

On rivers, there is a closed season between 15 March and 15 June inclusive. On canals and stillwaters, it is up to the landowner whether to enforce a closed season.

Sea fishing is different, you don't need any licences to fish in the sea, and there is no closed season.

US

In the US, rules are set on a state by state basis, with coastal states having one set for fresh water and another for salt water.

Some states have closed seasons but usually only for certain species, and with no differentiation between still and running water. Anglers are licenced rather than rods, with each state having a rule about how many rods an angler can use at once. Licences are available from all larger fishing shops, plus some other stores.

You are free to fish on almost any public land, but private land is by permission only. The water is not owned though, so if there is any public access to launch a boat, you have the freedom of the entire lake or river as long as you are on the water!

RULES

No fishing without a licence.

No fishing underneath power lines.

Do not leave any litter, and if you find any take it home with you!

Do not enter the water to get things you have dropped.

DIET & FITNESS

A lot of fishing is very active, and it's no coincidence that many of the best anglers are those who put a lot of effort into their fishing. You'll be surprised at how fit fishing keeps you!

A healthy balanced diet is important when fishing. You'll be doing lots of walking, tree climbing (where allowed) and creeping about, so you'll need energy from your food to keep you going. This pie chart shows you the percentages of foods that should be eaten to maintain a balanced diet.

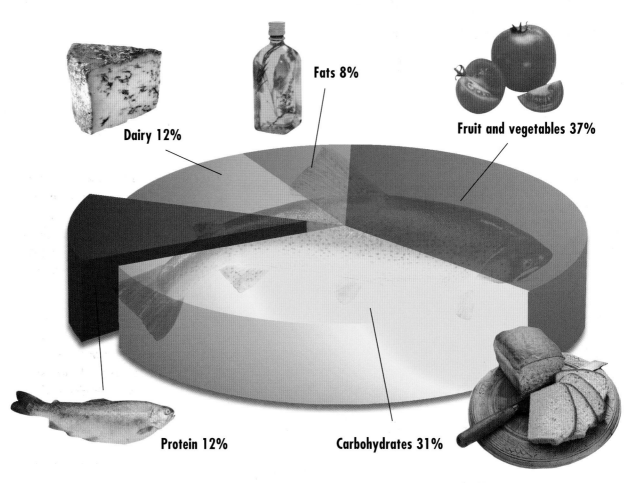

Dairy 12%

Fats 8%

Fruit and vegetables 37%

Protein 12%

Carbohydrates 31%

Always carry plenty of fresh water, especially in summer, and enough food for your session.

Sandwiches are ideal for keeping you full, and snacks like chocolate are useful for an energy boost. If you are night fishing, nothing beats a small stove for making hot food and drinks.

If you do a lot of fishing, invest in a good, adjustable chair.

SAFETY

Being in the middle of nature next to water can be risky, but as long as you're sensible there's no reason you should come to any harm. It's a good idea to go fishing with a friend or two — not just for safety but you'll need someone to photograph your new personal best for you! It's also worth taking a mobile phone, just in case you need to contact anyone. Some out-of-the-way places have limited network coverage though, so don't be completely reliant on it.

Tell at least one person where you're going and what time you'll be back. It only takes a few seconds but it might turn out to be very important.

If it's going to be dusk or dark when you come home, make sure you take a good torch and spare batteries, and walk carefully.

Be careful at the water's edge or when out in boats. It's possible to drown in just a few centimetres of water. If you do go out in a boat, always wear a lifejacket.

Finally, be aware of overhead power lines. Never fish directly underneath them. Carbon (which is what most rods are made of) is an excellent conductor of electricity, and a shock via a fishing rod is enough to kill. When walking under power lines, keep your rods parallel with the ground – a rod doesn't need to touch the lines to conduct the electricity. But as long as you're sensible, there's nothing to worry about.

Be aware of overhead power lines.

HOW THE FAMOUS DO IT

A *'successful' angler means different things to different people, whether that's winning lots of money in high-pressure fishing tournaments or patiently and carefully outwitting the biggest, craftiest fish. What good anglers have in common though is a thoughtful, individual approach. They have the ability to solve problems and pay close attention to the weather and conditions. However, if you go fishing and enjoy yourself, that's a success! Here are some of the most successful anglers.*

ROLAND MARTIN

Roland Martin is a professional US sport fisherman, fishing primarily for bass in tournaments.

He is very successful, having won many competitions and been invited into the Professional Bass Fishing Hall of Fame, the International Game Fish Association Hall of Fame and the Freshwater Fishing Hall of Fame. He also hosts the TV programme, 'Fishing with Roland Martin'.

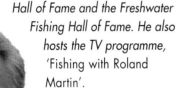

GEORGINA BALLANTYNE

Fishing is a great sport for men and women.

On 7 October 1922, Georgina Ballantyne caught the biggest salmon ever recorded in the UK – and it's still the record! The huge 64 lb River Tay fish took a fly, and it took 10 hours to land. It is reported that the salmon was so big a pony and cart was needed to get the fish home!

RICHARD WALKER

Thought to be the most influential angler in living memory, Richard (Dick) Walker revolutionised the sport.

He was the first person to say that big fish – especially carp – could be caught by design. Before him, carp were considered impossible to catch! There wasn't any specialised tackle when he started fishing, so he had to design and make his own, including bite alarms, rods, flies and Arlesey bomb weights. Some of his Mark IV split cane rods are still in use today, and are extremely expensive!

MATT HAYES

Matt Hayes is probably the UK's best-known fishing celebrity.

He was 30 when he gave up his successful office job to launch a career in fishing. He has fished all over the world and caught all kinds of fish, even Great White Sharks, but for him the mystery and excitement of fishing are more important than the size and weight of the catch. Matt won the Drennan Cup (specimen fishing's top prize) in 1998 but since then he has left big fish angling behind to explore different locations and methods of fishing.

GLOSSARY

BOBBIN - A method of bite indication. A bobbin clips and hangs on the line between the reel and rod rest, rising or falling when a fish takes the bait.

BOLT RIG - A leger rig using a heavy weight to cause fish to 'bolt' and hook themselves.

BITE ALARM - An electronic device which beeps when a fish pulls line over a small wheel or vibration sensor.

BOILIE - Flavoured and nutritious paste baits which are rolled into balls and boiled, and are often used for carp fishing.

BRAID - Main line or hooklength material which is very low diameter for its breaking strain and has no stretch. It is not very abrasion resistant however, so care should be taken if using around snags.

CASTING - Using a rod to throw bait or a fly into water.

CASTING WEIGHT - The total weight (made up of split-shot or leger weights) needed to cast the rig the required distance.

CLOSE-IN - Fishing close to the bank.

DISGORGER - A pencil-like item with a slit in one end. it is used to remove hooks.

DROPBACK - When legering, when a fish takes the bait and swims towards you, causing the bobbin to drop back instead of going up.

FORCEPS - An unhooking tool for pike and zander fishing.

GROUNDBAIT - A mix of crumb and cereals with flavours and additives, which is mixed with water to a fluffy consistency, squeezed together and thrown in the water to attract fish and encourage them to feed.

GROYNES - A low wall or sturdy timber barrier built out into the sea from a beach.

HAIR-RIG - A way of presenting a bait (often a boilie) so it is not directly on the hook, achieving more bites from wary fish and improved hooking. The bait is held on a short piece of line attached to the hook.

HOOKLENGTH - A length of line used to connect your hook to your main line.

LOOSEFEED - Bait that you can throw into the water to attract fish to feed in a certain area.

LURE - Any 'bait' which imitates natural, living creatures that fish eat.

MARGINS - The edge of a lake or river, often the best place to fish – if you're quiet!

MONOFILAMENT - Normal nylon fishing line.

PLUMMET - A special weight used to measure the depth when float fishing.

RUN RING - This has a wide bore allowing free passage of line so a fish can pull the line through without feeling resistance.

SPECIMEN - A large fish of a certain species.

SPLIT-SHOT - A small weight attached to the line when float fishing.

TAPERED LEADER - A length of monofilament line that is thick at one end and thin at the other end.

UNHOOKING MAT - A padded mat used to put fish on while they are being unhooked, to prevent them coming to harm on rough ground.

LISTINGS

Environment Agency

PO Box 544, Rotherham, S60 1BY, UK

Tel: +44 8708 506 506

Website: www.environment-agency.gov.uk

National Federation of Anglers

National Water Sports Centre, Adbolton Lane, Holme Pierrepont, Nottingham, NG12 2LU, UK

Tel: +44 115 981 3535

Website: www.nfadirect.com

American Fisheries Society

5410 Grosvenor Lane, Bethesda, MD 20814, USA

Tel: +1 (301) 897 8616

Website: www.fisheries.org/afs/index.html

American Sportfishing Association

225 Reinekers Lane, Suite 420, Alexandria, VA 22314, USA

Tel: +1 703 519 9691

Website: www.asafishing.org/asa/